Toothpaste Trouble
Poems from Breakfast to Bedtime

Nick Toczek is a poet with four best-selling
collections published by Macmillan Children's Books.
He is also a professional storyteller, magician,
puppeteer, journalist and stand-up comedian.
For more information on Nick Toczek, check out his
website at http://www.poems.fsnet.co.uk

Gerald Hawksley has illustrated lots of books, but he likes
illustrating poetry books best of all – because the pictures
are already there, in the poems. Gerald lives in Wiltshire
with his wife and daughter, a cat, a dog, and a small but
persistent goldfish.

Toothpaste Trouble

Poems from Breakfast to Bedtime

Chosen by Nick Toczek

Illustrated by Gerald Hawksley

MACMILLAN CHILDREN'S BOOKS

First published 2002
by Macmillan Children's Books
a division of Macmillan Publishers Ltd
20 New Wharf Road, London N1 9RR
Basingstoke and Oxford
www.panmacmillan.com

Associated companies throughout the world

ISBN 0 330 39753 2

5 7 9 8 6

A CIP catalogue record for this book is available from the British Library.

Printed by Mackays of Chatham plc, Chatham, Kent.

'Toothpaste Trouble' by Coral Rumble first published in *Hop to the Sky!* by Ginn and Company
1999. 'Out-time, In-time' by Brian Moses first published in *I Wish I Could Dine with a Porcupine*
by Hodder Children's Books 2000. 'Paintbox' by Mike Johnson first published in *Rhyme Time –
Around the Day* by Oxford University Press 2000. 'Whiz Kid' by Gina Douthwaite first published
in *Countdown* by Ginn and Company 1998. 'Little Red Van' by Sue Cowling first published in
Rhyme Time – Around the Day by Oxford University Press 2000. 'Your Friend the Sun' by Roger
McGough first published in *Sky in the Pie* by Puffin Books 1985. 'At the Top of the Stairs' by
Andrew Fusek Peters first published in *Sadderday and Funday* by Hodder Wayland 2001.
Reproduced by permission of Hodder and Stoughton Ltd. 'I luv Me Mudder' from *Wicked
World* by Benjamin Zephaniah (Puffin 2000). Text copyright © Benjamin Zephaniah, 2000.
Reproduced by permission of Penguin Books Ltd. 'Night Boy' by Matthew Sweeney first
published in *Up on the Roof* by Faber Children's Books 2001.

Contents

Wake Me Up

Rock, rock, bubbly jock,
I'll wake you up at ten o'clock.

But ten o'clock is far too soon!
Wake me up in the afternoon.

Traditional

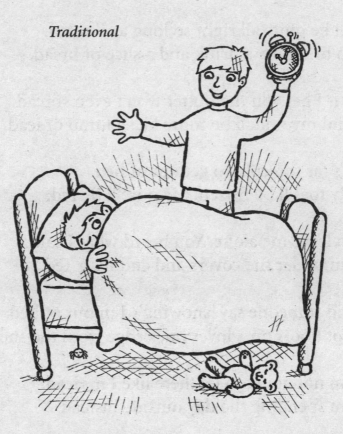

It's Freezing Cold

It's far too cold to get out of bed.
My toes'll be frozen. My nose'll be red.

I'll stay snuggled up all day instead.
You'll never see the top of my head.

I'll be quite all right so long as I'm fed.
So bring me a drink and a slice of bread.

But I bet you the butter won't even spread.
And my milk'll be more like a lump of lead.

It's far too cold to get out of bed.
My toes'll be frozen. My nose'll be red.

So leave me alone. You heard what I said.
I'm under the covers and cuddling Ted.

Did someone say 'snowing'? I'm out of bed.
Got boots on, gloves on, sledge from the shed.

I'm not going to lie there like I'm dead.
I'm spending the day outside instead.

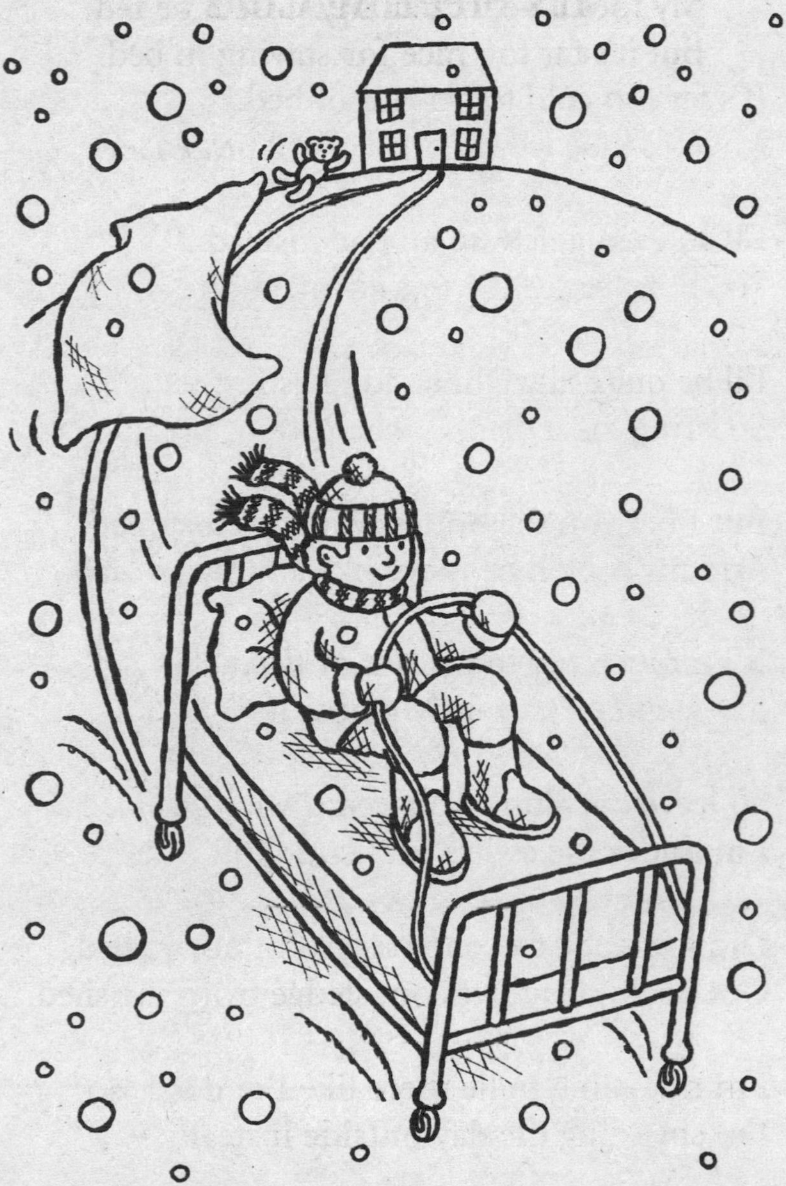

My toes'll be frozen. My nose'll be red.
But it's far too nice for staying in bed.

Nick Toczek

Toothpaste Trouble

I can use the flannel,
I can use the soap,
But when I use the toothpaste
I give up all hope.

I get
Toothpaste on my cheek,
Toothpaste on my nose,
Toothpaste on my ear,
Toothpaste on my clothes,
Toothpaste on my tummy,
Toothpaste on my knee,
And in lots of other places
That toothpaste shouldn't be!

Coral Rumble

Hair and Teeth and Face
and Hands

Get a little paste
Squeeze it on a brush
Rub it up and down
In a rush, rush, rush.
Don't forget your gums
And the difficult bit
Scrub it all around
And then spit, spit, spit.

Get a little sponge
Wet it in the sink
Rub it on your face
till you blink, blink, blink.
Don't forget your ears
Don't forget your neck
Rub it round your cheeks
And then check, check, check.

Get a little soap
Hold it in a grip
Rub it in your hands
Until they slip, slip, slip.
Don't forget the dirt
Don't forget the ink
Wash away the suds
In the sink, sink, sink.

Get a little comb
Pull it through with care
Straighten out the strands
Of your hair, hair, hair.
Don't forget the back
Don't forget the top
Make it look all neat
And then stop, stop, stop.

Steve Turner

Dressing

Trousers are a muddle.
How do they go on?
It's really such a struggle.
Where did I go wrong?

Whichever way I put my shirt
It's always outside in.
The sleeves get tangled and it hurts.
The buttons get my skin.

My socks get lost down my sleeves,
Stuck inside the ends.
The ankle's where the toe should be.
Oh, why so many bends?

They won't go on. My shoes won't help.
Oh, who put in that toy . . . ?
'Mummy, look. I've dressed myself.
Aren't I a clever boy!'

Susan Hardy-Dawson

Routes

1. The Walk to School

Down Barking-dog Lane
past the street with the boat
                    Clouds rush by
                    Sometimes it rains

Up Old-lady-waving Road
past the field with the car
                    Clouds hang still
                    Aeroplanes drone

Down Skateboard Steps
past the shop with the cat
                    Clouds make shapes
                    Reflect in windowpanes

2. The Drive to School

radio shouts
mum shouts
belt tight
window steam
dad shouts
radio shouts
feel hot
feel sick
radio, mum,
dad shout
shout shout
every day
same shout
same hot
same sick
same same
same same

Ian McMillan

Why Are You
Late for School?

I didn't get up
because I was too tired
and I was too tired
because I went to bed late
and I went to bed late
because I had homework
and I had homework
because the teacher made me
and the teacher made me
because I didn't understand
and I didn't understand
because I wasn't listening
and I wasn't listening
because I was staring out of the window
and I was staring out of the window
because I saw a cloud.
I am late, sir,
because I saw a cloud.

Steve Turner

Off to School

I had to go to school today
Although I'm only four.
I guess it means my parents
Just don't love me any more.

I should have seen it coming,
Seen the writing on the wall,
When they gave me books and pencils
And took away my ball.

The school was large and noisy
With children everywhere.
There must be lots of others
Who have parents who don't care.

Life is often very cruel,
And sometimes full of sorrow,
But the really awful thing is
I must go again tomorrow.

Brian D'Arcy

Bounce-a-ball

With my friends at playtime
  I play bounce-a-ball.
    It's bounce-a-ball to Emma
      and it's bounce-a-ball to Paul.
        It's bounce-a-ball to Ahmed
          and it's bounce-a-ball to Faz.
          It's bounce-a-ball to Guljit
        and it's bounce-a-ball to Jazz.
      It's bounce-a-ball to Stacey
    and it's bounce-a-ball to Matt.
It's bounce-a-ball to Sophie
  and it's bounce-a-ball to Pat.
    It's bounce-a-ball to Jeeta
      and it's bounce-a-ball to Luke.
        It's bounce-a-ball to Hannah
          and it's bounce-a-ball to Duke.
        It's bounce-a-ball to Chloe
      and it's bounce-a-ball to Wayne.
    It's bounce-a-ball to Amy
  and it's bounce-a-ball to Shane.
There goes the school bell
  and now our playtime ends.
    I played bounce-a-ball

with
   my
      best
         friends.

      Hey!

Wes Magee

I Like Playtime Because ...

A new girl's come to our school.
Her name is Tamsin Lee.
Miss Gray asked where she'd like to sit,
And she sat right next to me.

She wears her hair in tight black curls.
Her grin is five-miles-wide.
She sings like Björk, but *better*,
As she rocks from side to side.

And outside in the playground
She wants to play with *me*,
Not Bea, or Claire or Karen,
Not Harry, Rob or Dee.

We always play together,
And all the rest can see
That now I have a Best Friend –
Fantastic Tamsin Lee!

Jennifer Curry

Out-time, In-time

Out-time, out-time,
run around and shout time,
shake it all about time,
out-time, out-time.

In-time, in-time,
did you lose or win time,
chuck it in the bin time,
in-time, in-time.

Out-time, out-time,
have a knock about time,
give your friend a clout time,
out-time, out-time.

In-time, in-time,
it's time to begin time,
stop the noisy din time,
in-time, in-time.

Brian Moses

I Can . . .

Count to a hundred,
Read and write,
Draw a picture,
Fly a kite,
Rollerblade
Do a handstand,
Play a tune
With an elastic band,
Swim a length,
Multiply,
Kick a football
Play I-Spy,
Use a computer,
Tie my shoe,
I can do
Lots of things
– what about you?

Tony Langham

Really Really

I find it very hard to read.
So sometimes I pretend,
Just turning pages one by one
Until I reach the end.

Teacher tries to help me;
Knows just what I need.
Sounding words out one by one,
I really want to read.

I really, really want to read
Bright books there on the shelf.
I like it when Miss reads to me,
But I want to read myself.

I know there's magic locked in books,
Princes, places, birds.
That's why I try so very hard
To understand the words.

One day I know I'll really read
A book from start to end.
I won't just turn the pages.
I won't have to pretend.

John Kitching

Packed Lunches

While the school dinner-queue
Pushes and punches,
All of us pupils
With packed lunches
Sit around the playground
In small bunches.

Over each lunch-box
One of us hunches.
And, while the dinner-queue
Pushes and punches,
We chew cheese butties with
Munch-munch-munches,

Eat our apples with
Scrunch-scrunch-scrunches,
Gobble our crisps with
Crunch-crunch-crunches.
Meanwhile, the dinner-queue
pushes and punches.

We're all glad we
bring packed lunches.

Nick Toczek

Pencil World

Your pencil's amazing,
a magical stick.
It might make anything.
Take your pick:

a house on a hill
or a ship at sea,
a bus full of people,
a picture of me,

a fruit or a flower,
a battered old ball,
elephants, igloos,
anything at all.

Everything's in it,
tightly curled,
waiting to wake
from pencil world.

Tony Mitton

The Painting

I drew a picture of a lady
and coloured it with care
with round, green glasses on the nose
and lots of purple hair.
Then a big green smile with bright blue teeth
and a dress of orange-pink.
My teacher bent to take a look
and said, 'I'll have to think.
Could it be a monster or a
monkey from the zoo?'
'No,' I told her proudly,
'my picture is of you!'

Marian Swinger

Paintbox

Can't find blue,
but here is green.
The strangest coloured
sky I've seen.

Can't find yellow,
but here is white.
My brilliant sun's
a lovely sight.

Can't find brown,
but here is red.
I'll have to use
this shade, instead.

There, I've finished.
Come and see!
Green Sky, white sun
and bright red me.

Mike Johnson

Paying Attention

Yes!
Absolutely!
Right away!
Okie-dokie!

Affirmative!
Correct!
Right on!
Spiffing!

I agree!
I concur!
You are SO correct!
But . . . what was it you said?

Thom The Poet

Whiz Kid

Beth's the best at reading,
Gary's good at sums,
Kirsty's quick at counting
On her fingers and her thumbs.

Wayne's all right at writing,
Charles has lots of chums
But I'm the fastest out of school
When home time comes.

Gina Douthwaite

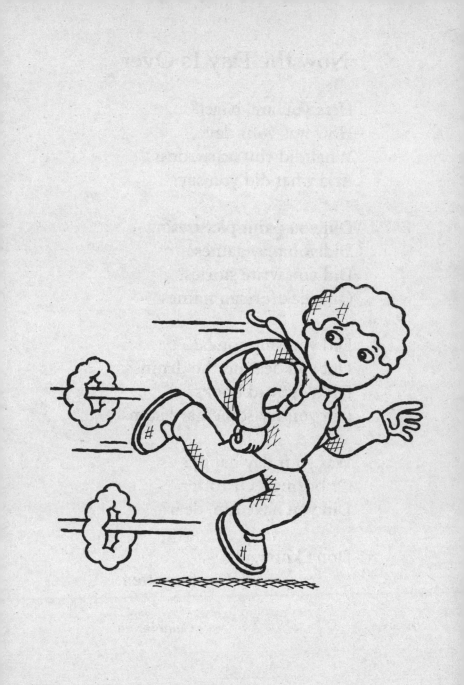

Now the Day Is Over

Here you are, Nigel!
How was your day?
What did you learn, dear?
And what did you say?

Did you paint pictures?
Did you play games?
Did you write stories?
Or speak foreign names?

Did you sing songs?
Did you beat on the drums?
Did you read books?
Did you try some hard sums?

Was your day happy?
Or boring? Or rotten?
Did you have fun, dear?

Don't know.
                    I've forgotten.

Clare Bevan

My House

Will you come
  to MY house
and stay, and have
  some tea?

It's got a number
  on the gate:
number
  twenty-three.

Ask your Mum
  to bring you,
and give the door
  a knock:

Come inside
  and play with me
and stay
  till six o'clock.

Jean Kenward

Walking

My socks have slipped down in my wellies
and I don't like walking through mud.
'Mum, my feet hurt. How much further?'

I'm all sweaty so I pull off my cagoule
although it's raining cats and dogs.
'My back's itchy, Mum. How much further?'

I'm really hungry and ever so thirsty
and I wish I'd eaten more for breakfast.
'Mum, it must be time for lunch. How much
further?'

I wouldn't mind walking if we had a dog.
My friend Pete got a dog last Christmas.
'Couldn't we have a dog, Mum? Or a cat, even.
How much further?

I can't think of anything else
and I know Mum isn't listening
and I can tell from the way she is walking that
there's still miles and miles and miles . . .

Liz Cashdan

Sticky Shadows

My sticky shadow
sticks to my feet,
as I go walking
down the street.

Left-right-left,
it keeps in time,
and even if
I climb
a tree,
my sticky shadow
sticks with me;

no matter how
I jump and shout,
my shadow follows
all about;
I shake my feet,
or go tip-toe;
my sticky shadow *won't* let go!

John Cunliffe

Vice-Versa

I smell with my nose,
And I run with my feet;
I know this very well.
But, I've noticed that sometimes
My nose starts to run,
And my feet begin to smell!

Mike Jubb

Look After Him

I've had to watch my brother
While our mum's been up the shops . . .
He's been playing down the garden,
All this time – but now he stops,
And stands still – as if he's thought of
Some peculiar idea . . .
And when he gets his brainwaves
Sisters shouldn't interfere!

'I stand here in the garden
And I realize I am *three*!
On one side is the garden fence,
On one side is a tree,
Our cat is in the peonies,
And I think it's going to rain,
And if it's wet this afternoon
Can I still come out again?'

Alan Brownjohn

Corner Shop

The corner shop
is full of tins
and vegetables in wire bins
and breakfast packets on a shelf
and sweets where you can help yourself.

The corner shop
has videos
and chocolates with big red bows.
My favourite bit is still the shelf
with sweets where you can help yourself.

Jill Townsend

In the Supermarket

Frozen peas,
Cheddar cheese,
A tin of Spam,
Strawberry jam,

A pound of steak,
A cherry cake,
Chocolate mousse,
Orange juice,

Instant coffee,
Creamy toffee,
Tins of beans,
A pair of jeans,

A potted plant,
Toy elephant,
A garden trowel,
A bath towel,

Shampoo,
Special glue,
A clothes line,
Red wine.

Fresh eggs,
Plastic pegs,
Leg of lamb,
Boiled ham . . .

Eek! And only half
Way down her list!
Already thinking
What she's missed!

Such a jam-packed
Trolley-load of stuff!
Crikey, Ma,
Enough's enough!

Matt Simpson

Little Red Van

Mum, can I have a ride?
It's only 30p.
I can drive the little red van
And you can wave to me.

Dad, can I have a ride?
It's two for 50p.
I can sing the postman's song
And you can sing with me.

Nan, can I have a ride?
It's five goes for a pound.
You come too and be the cat
That helps me do my round!

Sue Cowling

When It's Wet

There are things that I can't do
WHEN IT'S WET
I get soaked through and through
WHEN IT'S WET
I leave puddles in the hall
So I can't go out at all
It's worse than being at school
WHEN IT'S WET

I have to stay indoors
WHEN IT'S WET
And I get awfully bored
WHEN IT'S WET
Painting pictures is OK
But not for all the day
And they're no good anyway
WHEN IT'S WET

My coat hangs on the door
WHEN IT'S WET
Damp from the day before
WHEN IT'S WET
And there are hamsters to be fed
And the rabbits in the shed
I feel like staying in bed
WHEN IT'S WET

I can do things that I like
NOW IT'S DRY
I can go out on my bike
NOW IT'S DRY
Take my skateboard to the park
Play football
Have a lark
I'll stay out till it's dark
NOW IT'S DRY

John Row

Your Friend the Sun

Your friend the sun
came round to call
You kept him waiting
in the hall
And as the afternooon wore on
two – three – four
and he was gone

Roger McGough

Don't

Don't comb your hair in company.
Don't cross the kitchen floor in welly boots.
Don't put the television on.
Don't squint. Don't get in fights.

Don't stuff your mouth with sausage.
Don't drop towels on the bathroom floor.
Don't hang about with that rough crowd.
Don't put your feet up on the chair.

Don't use up all the paper in the loo.
Don't scratch. Don't twitch. Don't sniff. Don't
  talk.
Don't stick your tongue out.
Don't you dare to answer back.

Life is full of opportunity, says my mum.

Barrie Wade

Wasn't Me

There's a person in our house
No one can ever see.
He's the naughtiest and noisiest.
His name is Wasn't Me.

I know he'll be about
As soon as trouble stirs
Cos he eats all the biscuits
And drops things down the stairs.

He chucks our shoes and coats about.
He always spills his tea.
It's him who loses everything:
That nuisance, Wasn't Me.

He's the one who gets the toys out,
Tears paper into bits,
Throws the felt-tips on the floor,
And never puts on lids.

Mum always seems to miss him
But whoever's there, you see,
When she asks nicely: 'Who did this?'
It's always 'Wasn't Me!'

Susan Hardy-Dawson

At the Top of the Stairs

I live at the top of the stairs,
The safest place to be,
Especially when there's an argument
In my stormy family.

It starts off in the living room.
It isn't very polite.
Their whisper grows into thunder.
I'm glad I'm out of sight.

I hate it when they shout.
It fills me up with gloom.
I hope the hurricane stays below
As I run to be safe in my room.

I think they forget about me,
And my space at the top of the stairs.
Oh, when will the storm blow over?
I wonder if anyone cares.

Andrew Fusek Peters

I Luv Me Mudder

I luv me mudder an me mudder luvs me
We cum so far from over de sea,
We heard dat de streets were paved wid gold
Sometimes it's hot, sometimes it's cold,
I luv me mudder an me mudder luvs me
We try fe live in harmony
Yu might know her as Valerie
But to me she's just my mummy.

She shouts at me daddy so loud sometime
She's always been a friend of mine
She's always doing de best she can
She works so hard down ina Englan,
She's always singin sum kinda song
She has big muscles an she very, very strong,
She likes pussycats an she luvs cashew nuts
An she don't bother wid no if an buts.

I luv me mudder an me mudder luvs me
We come so far from over de sea,
We heard dat de streets were paved wid gold
Sometimes it's hot, sometimes it's cold,
I luv her and whatever we do
Dis is a luv I know is true,
My people, I'm talking to yu
Me an my mudder we luv yu too.

Benjamin Zephaniah

Bouncing with
the Budgie

Budgie's bouncing,
Kitten's pouncing,
Dog is fast asleep,
Mum is trusting
Dad with the dusting,
Cooker's going Beep!

Budgie's singing,
Telephone's ringing,
Sister's going out.
My room's tidy
And it's Friday
So I want to shout:

Budgie, go on bouncing!
Kitten, give me five!
Dog, wake up and play with me!
Weekend, come alive!

Celia Warren

Home

The lamp is on
in my little house.
The table is set
for tea.
My slippers are there
beside the fire
and they're waiting
just for me.

The cat's curled up
in her basket.
The coals glow gold
and red.
So soon I'll take
my storybook
and climb the stairs
to bed.

Tony Mitton

A Rubber Duck Song

Soft soap, toothpaste,
Big towel and flannel,
If I'm not in the bath
Then I'm swimming the channel.

So don't run the taps
Until I get back,
Shampoo, talcum
And quack quack quack.

John Mole

Into the Bathtub

Into the bathtub,
Great big splosh.
Toes in the bathtub,
Toes in the wash.

Soap's very slidy,
Soap smells sweet.
Soap all over,
Soap on your feet.

Rinse all the soap off,
Dirt floats away.
Dirt in the water.
Water's gone grey.

Out of the bathtub,
Glug, glug, glug.
Great big towel,
Great big hug.

Wendy Cope

A Bedtime Snack

To bed, to bed,
says Sleepy-head.
Let's bide a while, says Slow.
Put on the pot,
says Greedy-gut.
We'll sup before we go.

Traditional

Time for Bed for Teddy and Me

One step up
two steps up,
three steps up,
then comes four.
Five steps up,
six steps up,
seven steps up
and one more.
Nine steps up,
ten steps up.
Eleven steps up
to my bedroom door.
It's a long way up to go.
I'm all changed and ready
but I really am a sleepyhead
I forgot to bring up Teddy.
One step down,
two steps down,
three steps down,
I've had him since I was four.
Five steps down,
six steps down,

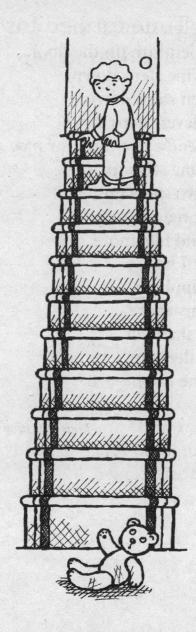

seven steps down,
I left him on the floor.
Nine steps down,
ten steps down,
eleven steps down,
Teddy give me your paw.
One step up,
two steps up,
three steps up
and lots more.
If I have to
climb up
any more
I shall fall
asleep on
the floor.

Janis Priestley

Looking for My Teddy

I'm looking for my teddy.
    Is he over there?
Has he fallen underneath
    My daddy's chair?

        No.

I'm looking for my teddy.
    Is he by the door?
Did I drop him on the stairs?
    I'll look there once more.

        No.

I'm looking for my teddy.
    Is he in the shed?
No.
        Oh!

            Mum! I've found my teddy

Snuggled down my bed!

Fred Sedgwick

Count-up to Planet Bed

I'm one for the window
and two for the door.

I'm three for the ceiling
and four for the floor.

I'm five for the morning
and six for the night.

I'm seven for the stairs
and eight for the light.

I'm nine for a story
and ten for my bed.

Now I'm off for a dream
to hold in my head.

Katherine Gallagher

Saying Goodnight

Pop pop poppa pop
Up the stairs we come
Puff puff puffa puff
The train's coming home.
Wooff wooff wooffa woof
Here comes the dog
Bringing mud all up the stairs
From the neighbour's bog.

Silkily and slinkily
The cat we hardly heard.
Flap flappa flappa flap
Out flies the bird.

Up comes Grandad with his stick
Bump bumpa bump
With something for the dog to lick
Schlump schlumpa schlump.

Everyone comes to say goodnight.
Kiss, and go to sleep;
Draw the curtain. Down we go
Creep   creep   creep.

Jenny Joseph

Bedtime March-past

I need to cuddle Penguin.
I need to cuddle Sheep.
I need to cuddle Crocodile
before I go to sleep.

I need to cuddle Little Bear,
then tuck him out of sight,
before I kiss old Dinosaur
who sometimes likes to fight.

I need to cuddle Monster,
then hide beneath the heap.
Mum says it's hard to find me
when toys lie seven-deep.

I need to cuddle Cattypus
before I put out the light.
But last of all I kiss my mum
and *then* I say 'Goodnight.'

Moira Andrew

Midnight

Sleep is another country
I visit in my head.
I watch my brother sleeping now –
His eyelids heavy-smooth as lead . . .
A million miles away from me
Across our bedroom, in his bed.

It feels as if there's only me,
I'm the last boy left alive,
After the end of everything –
The last one to survive . . .
The screech owl cries, the wild wolf howls
The whole wide world's an ache.

For I am the last and lonely one
The only one left awake.

Jan Dean

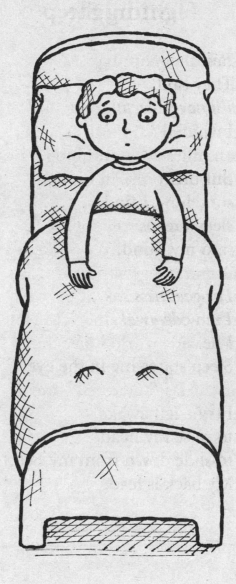

Fighting Sleep

Bed!
They said.
I'll never sleep!
I whined . . .

But then,
somehow, I find
sleep creeps
into my mind.

For goodness sake,
I'm wide awake!
I lie.
Sleep stares me in the eye.

I try
to raise my head,
to slide down from my bed.
My back is lead.

N – O – W!
sleep sighs
and gently closes
both my eyes.

Judith Nicholls

I Will Not Fall Asleep

Last night as I lay in my bed
A warm and cosy heap
I made a promise to myself
That I *would not* fall asleep.

Yes, I made myself a promise
I truly meant to keep
That no matter what might happen
I would not fall asleep.

I'd count the minutes on the clock
I'd listen to the cars
I'd do long divisions in my head
And add up all the stars.

I'd make my ears keep listening hard
Speak sharply to my eyes
And tell them not to dare to close
'Till they saw the sun arise.

And I wondered what they'd say at school
When I told them during break
That while they all lay fast asleep
I was wide awake.

I'd tell them all, 'It's easy.
All you do is keep
Both your eyes stuck open wide
And you'll never fall asleep.'

'No, you'll never fall asleep,' I'd say,
'Your eyes will never droop
If you keep on saying to yourself
I will not fall asloop.'

'Yes, never ever sloop a fall
Always wape akeep
If you keep on selfing to your say
I will
not fall
I will not fall
I
will
not fall
A z z z z z z z z z z z z z z z z z z z z z
Zzzzzzzzzzzzzzzzzzzzzzzzzzzzzzzzzzzzzzzzzzzz'

Gareth Owen

Night Boy

After the cat went out
and the moon sat on the hill
and the sea drowned a lorry
that broke down
       stealing sand,
little, skinny George awoke.

He was little, because he hardly grew.
He hardly grew, because he ate
scraps of chicken, leftover rice, dry bread,
what was left on the dog's plate,
handfuls of cornflakes, jam.
That may sound a lot
but it left George little and skinny.

What about mealtimes? I hear you ask.
Mealtimes, for George, were sleeptimes
most of the year. That's right,
he slept all day,
       got up at night.

What about school? you're saying.
I know, I know what you're like.
What do you know about stars?
Does the sea glow at night
like a green watch-dial?
Ask George, he'll tell you.
He'll even write it down
and read it to you, by torchlight,
and then he'll count the stars.

Blame the holidays, his Gran said,
they're too long.
George lived with his Gran,
George, the sleeper-in
who'd slept in so long, so often,
that now he woke at night
when Gran was asleep.

What did he do at night?
He went to the beach,
lit driftwood fires,
stood in a cave and waited
for spies in submarines
to land.
        He climbed hills
and aeroplane-spotted,
especially small ones
landing in fields.

He hid in ditches
and eavesdropped on strangers.
He woke the neighbour's donkey
and galloped round the field.

He lay on a haystack
and watched the dawn.
Then he yawned
        and went to bed.

And if he met Gran on the stairs,
Good day, was what he said.

Matthew Sweeney

Spectacular Spooks

Poems by Brian Moses

Spectacular Spooks is packed with incredible ghosts and
ghouls of all kinds. Meet the Teflon Terror,
beware the Night Creatures, do the Skeleton Hop,
find out what happens on Wilderness Hill and
much, much more . . .

Who's Afraid?

Do I have to go haunting tonight?
The children might give me a fright.
It's dark in that house.
I might meet a mouse.
Do I have to go haunting tonight?

I don't like the way they scream out,
When they see me skulking about.
I'd rather stay here,
Where there's nothing to fear.
Do I have to go haunting tonight?

John Foster

A selected list of poetry books available from Macmillan

The prices shown below are correct at the time of going to press. However, Macmillan Publishers reserve the right to show new retail prices on covers which may differ from those previously advertised.

Wacky Wild Animals	0 330 39205 0
Poems chosen by Brian Moses	£3.99
Magnificent Machines	0 330 39145 3
Poems chosen by John Foster	£3.99
Freaky Families	0 330 39207 7
Poems chosen by David Orme	£3.99
Spectacular Spooks	0 330 39206 9
Poems chosen by Brian Moses	£3.99
Poems for Five Year Olds	0 330 48303 X
Poems chosen by Susie Gibbs	£3.99
Poems for Six Year Olds	0 330 37181 9
Poems chosen by Susie Gibbs	£3.99
Ye New Spell Book	0 330 39708 7
Poems chosen by Brian Moses	£3.99

All Macmillan titles can be ordered at your local bookshop or are available by post from:

Book Service by Post
PO Box 29, Douglas, Isle of Man IM99 1BQ

Credit cards accepted. For details:
Telephone: 01624 675137
Fax: 01624 670923
E-mail: bookshop@enterprise.net

Free postage and packing in the UK.
Overseas customers: add £1 per book (paperback)
and £3 per book (hardback).